# Bunnies

Tone Finnanger

David and Charles

A DAVID & CHARLES BOOK

Copyright © J.W. Cappelens Forlag, AS 2010
Cappelen Hobby
www.cappelen.no

First published in the UK in 2010 by David & Charles
Reprinted in 2011, 2013, 2014, 2016, 2017, 2018

David & Charles is an imprint of F&W Media International, Ltd
Pynes Hill Court, Pynes Hill, Exeter, EX2 5AZ

F&W Media International, Ltd is a subsidiary of F+W Media, Inc
10151 Carver Road, Suite #200, Blue Ash, OH 45242, USA

Content and images first published in *Crafting Tilda's Friends*, *Sew Sunny
Homestyle*, *Sew Pretty Homestyle*, *Sew Pretty Christmas Homestyle*, *Crafting
Springtime Gifts* and *Crafting Christmas Gifts*.

A catalogue record for this book is available from the British Library.

ISBN-13: 978-0-7153-3873-5 hardback
ISBN-10: 0-7153-3873-0 hardback

Printed in China by RR Donnelley
for F&W Media International, Ltd
Pynes Hill Court, Pynes Hill, Exeter, EX2 5AZ

**Publisher** Ali Myer
**Acquisitions Editor** Jennifer Fox-Proverbs
**Assistant Editor** Jeni Hennah
**Project Editor** Beth Dymond
**Design Manager** Sarah Clark
**Production Controller** Bev Richardson
**Pre Press** Jodie Culpin

F+W Media publish high quality books on a wide range of subjects.
For more great book ideas visit: **www.sewandso.co.uk**

*www.ilovetilda.com*
*For beauty and inspiration in everything Tilda*

# CONTENTS

# Fabrics and Materials

## Fabrics

Fabrics with a slightly coarse weave are better for making stuffed figures than thin or fine fabrics, as they are much firmer and therefore easier to mould. Linen and plain cotton fabrics are the best types to use, and fabrics with a woven pattern are often preferable to printed patterns. If you would like to use thinner fabrics, you may find it useful to iron a layer of fusible interfacing on the wrong side, to give you a firmer fabric.

When choosing material for the skin colour, use pale linen to create a fair skin tone and light brown linen for darker skin tones. If you are making animals, try using a material with stripes or spots to create an interesting fur effect.

The designs that do not require stuffing, as well as the clothes for the figures and the appliqué projects, can be made from cottons, polyester cottons and most types of fabric. These can therefore be much more decorative than the fabrics used for the stuffed figures.

Fabrics can be bought from craft shops, patchwork and quilting suppliers, and even some department stores. You could also try shops that sell fabrics for curtains and upholstery, which are often a good source for classic patterns and French Toile.

## Stuffing

For the projects in this book you will need a good-quality polyester stuffing to fill the figures. A selection of stuffing and wadding can be purchased from most patchwork and quilting shops, as well as from many online retailers.

# Fusible interfacing

Fusible interfacing comes in various thicknesses to suit different projects. Volume interfacing is an iron-on fusible wadding (batting) that produces a firm, padded result. Lightweight interfacing is much thinner and is used for stiffening or reinforcing lighter fabrics. Firm interfacing is used for making fabric boxes and large bags, so that the items will stand upright without collapsing. For the best results, choose a fusible interfacing that is slightly lighter in weight than your fabric.

# Iron-on adhesive

Bondaweb is a strong double-sided adhesive, which bonds one fabric to another when ironed. The adhesive side is pressed against the reverse side of a material and the paper is torn off, resulting in an adhesive material for simple appliqué work. You can also buy Wonderweb iron-on tape, which is useful for attaching smaller pieces of fabric, such as adding trims.

# Accessories

A huge variety of beads, ribbons, buttons and other embellishments can be found in craft shops, or you can collect natural materials to decorate your projects. Tilda products, such as mini gold crowns and dolls' hair, are available from www.pandurohobby.co.uk.

# Useful tools

- A vanishing ink pen
  Useful for tracing patterns onto fabric. The line disappears when you press it with a damp cloth or after a short while. Alternatively, you can use a fine waterproof fabric pen, or a white gel roller-ball pen for darker fabrics.
- Small pointed fabric scissors
  Vital for getting precise shapes when cutting out material.
- A transparent sewing machine foot
  Makes it easier to see and follow the pattern that has been traced onto the fabric.
- A wooden plant stick
  Useful for turning figures the right way out and inserting stuffing.
- Craft paints
  Used for creating faces for the figures and adding details to the clothes and accessories.

# Templates

All templates at the back of this book need to be enlarged by 400%. Add seam allowance for all templates, unless otherwise stated.

For details of craft shops and suppliers, please refer to the list on page 46.

# Stuffed Forms

## Faces

It is always best to wait until the ears and any headdresses are in place before you add the face. This makes it easier for you to see where the eyes should be positioned. Insert two pins in the head where the eyes should be. Remove the pins and fix the eyes in the pinholes, using the eye tool from a face kit or the head of a pin dipped in black paint. Blusher or lipstick can be applied with a dry brush to create rosy cheeks.

## Noses

Noses for bunnies and hares are sewn with pink thread as shown in Figure A. All kinds of thread can be used and the number of stitches depends on the threads chosen.

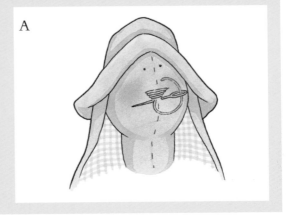

A

### SEWING

Avoid cutting out the item first unless absolutely necessary. Fold the fabric double, right sides facing, and transfer the pattern to it. Mark any openings for reversing indicated on the pattern. Sew carefully and evenly along the marked lines, using a stitch length of 1.5–2mm (⅝–¾in).

### CUTTING OUT

Cut out the item with a narrow seam allowance of 3–4mm (⅛in). Where there are openings for reversing, cut a wider seam allowance of about 7–8 mm (⁵⁄₁₆in). Cut a notch in the seam allowance where the seam curves sharply inwards.

## REVERSING

A pointed wooden garden cane or stick is useful for reversing. Use mainly the blunt end, except for details such as the bill on a bird where you can use the sharp end to carefully push it out. To avoid the stick poking through the fabric, trim the tip slightly to make it less sharp.

To reverse long, thin shapes, such as legs and arms, push the blunt end of the stick against the foot, see Figure B. Start close to the foot and pull the leg down along the stick, see Figure C. Continue to pull the leg down the stick until the tip/foot emerges from the opening. Pull the foot while drawing back the bottom so that the leg turns right side out, see Figure D.

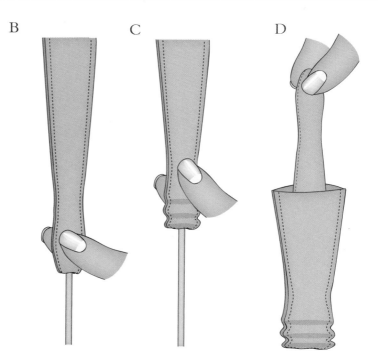

B          C          D

## STUFFING

Fold in the extra seam allowance along the opening in the seam. Press the item.

Use your fingers where you can when you are stuffing. Where your fingers won't fit, use the blunt end of a pen or pencil; it will only break through the stuffing and fabric if the tool is too thin.

Push the filling loosely into the item; avoid compressing it into a solid mass before it is in position. Push the filling carefully but firmly into place, adding more filling until you have a firm and well-shaped form. Sew up the opening neatly.

# SUMMER TREAT

## YOU WILL NEED

- *Fabric for the body, head, tummy patch, ice cream cone and ice cream*
- *Stuffing*
- *Buttons for attaching the arms*
- *A pompom for the tail*
- *Stranded embroidery thread (floss) for the nose*
- *Paint and blusher or lipstick for the face*
- *Small red fabric ball or bead for the ice cream*
- *Mini gold crown*

## HOW TO MAKE
### BODY
Read the section on 'Stuffed Forms' on pages 8–9 before starting.

The body is composed of three parts: two back parts and one front part. Fold the fabric for the back parts double, right sides facing, and transfer the pattern. Sew along the outline between the two points marked A and B on the pattern, but leaving the opening for reversing. Cut out.

Make different flavours of ice-cream by varying the colour of the fabric.

Transfer the pattern for the front part to a single layer of fabric, sew around the outline and cut out. Fold out the back part, put it against the front part, right sides facing, making sure that the edges are matching, see Figure A, and sew together.

Trim the surplus seam allowance, turn right side out and press. Stuff the body. Slip stitch together the opening for reversing.

Fold a piece of fabric for the head, arms and ears, and a contrasting piece of fabric for the tummy patch, double, right sides facing. Transfer the pattern pieces, sew around the outlines and cut out. Fold the opening at the top of the head the opposite way so that the seams are aligning. Sew up the opening, see Figure B.

A

B

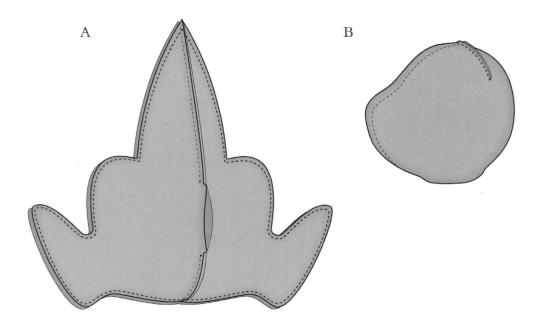

Make openings for reversing through one fabric layer on the arms and tummy patch. Make sure that the openings on the arms are on opposite sides on each arm so that you have a left and a right arm. Turn the head, arms, ears and tummy patch, right side out.

Fold in the seam allowance around the openings. Press and stuff the arms, head and ears. Put the head opening over the neck and slip stitch the head to the body. Slip stitch the tummy patch and the ears to the body as well.

Use buttons and embroidery thread (floss) to attach the arms tightly to the body, see Figure C. Sew a pompom to the bunny for a tail.

C

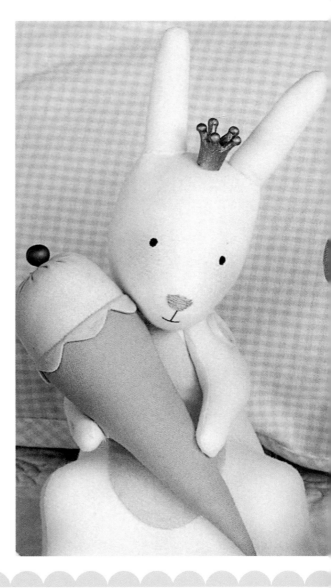

## FACE

Sew on the nose using pink embroidery thread (floss). Make the mouth by using black embroidery thread (floss) and sewing a stitch straight down from the nose and then a stitch across (see photo). Add the eyes and rosy cheeks, following the instructions on page 8, and attach the crown if desired.

## ICE CREAM

To make the ice cream, place the fabric for the cone and the fabric for the ice cream together, right sides facing.

Transfer the pattern to the fabric and sew along the scalloped top edge, see Figure D. Cut out, adding a seam allowance. Cut a notch in the seam allowance between each curve.

D

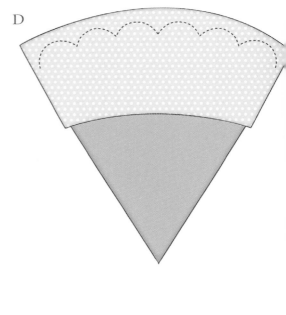

Lift up the ice cream. Fold the whole ice cream cone double, right sides facing. Sew together down the side, see Figure E.

Trim the surplus seam allowance, turn the ice cream cone right side out and then turn the scallops right side out. Push the ice cream part down into the cone part and top stitch around the top edge, just below the scallops, see Figure F.

Lift the ice cream part back up and fold in the edge around the opening. Stuff the ice cream. Sew running stitches around the opening, pull to gather and stitch to close, see Figure G. Attach a red fabric ball or bead to the top.

Sew the ice cream cone to the bunny to finish.

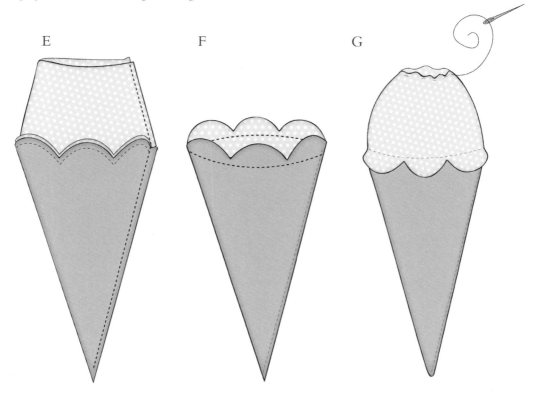

E    F    G

# ON THE FARM

<table>
<tr>
<td>

## YOU WILL NEED
- *Fabric for the body, nose, clothes and carrot*
- *Iron-on interfacing*
- *Stuffing*
- *Water-based craft paints*
- *Root threads*

</td>
<td>

## HOW TO MAKE

### BODY

Read the section on 'Stuffed Forms' on pages 8–9 before starting.

Cut out the three body parts and the parts for the arms and ears from the pattern. Put the two similar pieces right sides together and sew around, see Figure A. Fold out and put the piece you have just sewn together against the back piece. Hold the edges together with pins, see Figure B.

</td>
</tr>
</table>

A

B

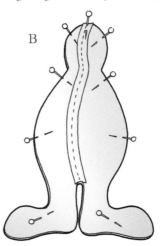

> This bunny is wearing dungarees but you can choose to make a dress instead (see page 19).

16

Sew the arms, turn them right side out and stuff.
Sew around the figure and attach the arms by
sewing up the opening. Put the parts for ears
right sides together and sew around, see Figure
C. Turn the ears right side out and iron. Turn the
body right side out and stuff. Tack (baste) the legs
together so the rabbit can stand. Wrinkle the ears
a little bit at the centre before you sew them on,
see Figure D.

### FACE
Dip a pin head in black water-based paint and
push it against the face to create the eyes. If you
find this difficult, you can also draw on small eyes
with a waterproof pen. To make the nose, iron
interfacing to the reverse side of the fabric. Tear
the paper away, cut out a little triangle for the
nose and iron on to the face.

### ANIMAL PRINT EFFECT
If you want to add an animal print effect, you can
easily paint spots or stripes onto the fabric once
the body has been sewn together.

Add some water-based craft paint to a small
amount of water and mix together. Try out the
colour on a test piece so you can see how much
the colour bleeds into the surface. Ensure you
leave enough space between the stripes or dots
to prevent them bleeding into each other.

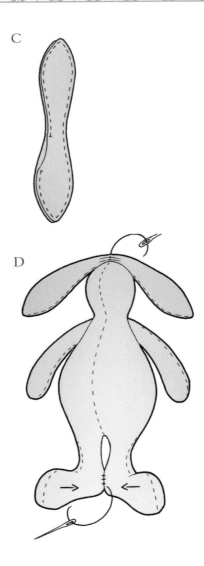

C

D

## CLOTHES

You can choose to make a dress (see below) or dungarees (see page 20) for your bunny to wear.

E

F

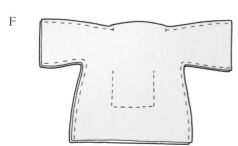

G

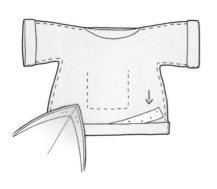

## DRESS

Cut out the parts for the dress and the pocket from the pattern. Iron the seam allowance along the edges of the pocket, and sew it on to the right side of one of the dress parts, as marked on the pattern, see Figure E.

Put the two parts for the dress right sides together and sew around, see Figure F. Cut out some thin strips of interfacing and tear off the paper. Fold in the seam allowance at the bottom of the dress, on the arms and around the neck.

Put the interfacing into the folds and iron, see Figure G. Turn the dress right side out. Iron again.

## DUNGAREES

Cut out the parts for the trousers, and two strips for braces measuring 4 × 14cm (1½ × 5½in) plus seam allowances. Put the parts for the trousers right sides together and fold the strips for the braces in two. Sew around, see Figure H. Fold in the seam allowance around the legs and the opening on top of the trousers.

Iron with interfacing in the same way as for the dress. Turn the dungarees right sides out and use a stick to turn out the braces. Put the trousers on the figure and fold in two pleats at the front and back so the trousers are tight. Attach with pins.

Tack (baste) the braces to the inside of the back of the trousers, see Figure I. Attach the braces outside the trousers and sew two buttons in front, see Figure J.

*For an alternative look, use plain brown linen for the face and body and striped fabric for the dungarees.*

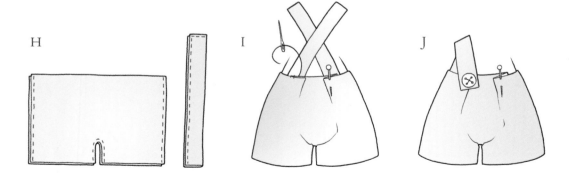

H                    I                    J

## SUN HAT

Cut out the parts for the hat using the pattern. Put the parts right sides together and sew around, see Figure K. Turn the hat right side out and iron. Push the piece with the reversing opening into the other part, see Figure L. Fold out the brim and iron, see Figure M.

## CARROT

Cut out the pieces for the carrot from the pattern. Put the parts right sides together and sew around, see Figure N. Turn right side out and stuff. Fold in the seam allowance around the opening on the top and sew along the border. Push in some root threads before you gather the opening, see Figure O.

K

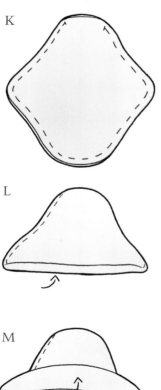

L

M

N 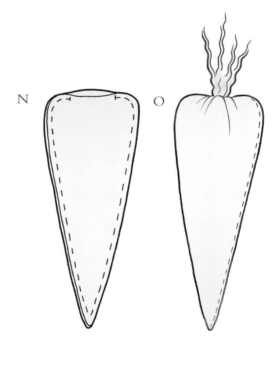 O

# LAZY DAYS

## YOU WILL NEED

- *Dark or light brown linen for the body*
- *Fabric for lining ears and clothes*
- *Stuffing*
- *Embroidery threads and fabric paints for the face and clothes*

## HOW TO MAKE

### BODY

Read the section on 'Stuffed Forms' on pages 8–9 before starting.

Fold the linen double and trace round the patterns for the body (once) and arms and legs (twice).

There are different patterns for making the smaller and larger sized bunnies.

Sew around the pieces leaving ends open, see
Figure A.
Place the linen fabric and the ear lining fabric
right sides together, trace the ear shape and sew
around it, leaving an opening, see Figure B.

Cut out all the pieces, turn inside out and press.
Stitch the ear opening. Stuff the body, arms and legs.

Insert the legs into the end of the body and sew
up the opening to fasten the legs. Then stitch the
arms to the body and the ears, lining side down, to
the head, see Figure C.

C

A

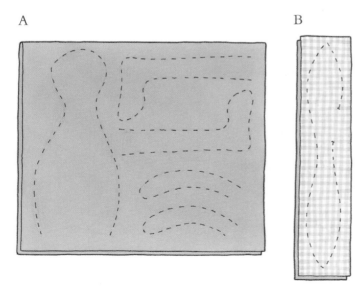

B

## FACE

Dip the head of a sewing pin into black paint to create eyes and stitch a nose with pink thread, see Figure D. You can also add rosy cheeks by applying colour with a brush. If the bunny is to wear a hat, you may want to postpone adding the face until the hat is in place.

## PANTALOONS

Fold the fabric in half and place the straight edge of the pattern piece on the fold. Cut out two pieces for the pantaloons, adding extra seam allowance at the waist and at the bottom of the legs.

Place the two pieces with right sides together, and sew the centre seams, see Figure E.

If you want machine embroidery at the bottom of the legs, fold up the hem and use the embroidery to fasten it before you sew the leg seam. Make sure the embroidery is on the right side, see Figure F.

If you do not want any embroidery, or if you are adding hand-sewn decorations, leave the hems until you have sewn up the trouser legs.

D

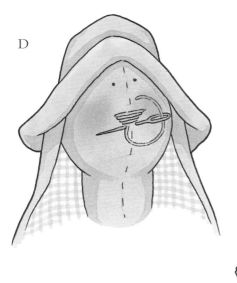

E

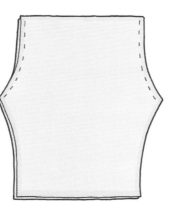
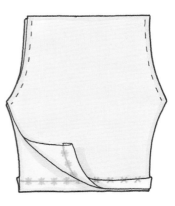

G

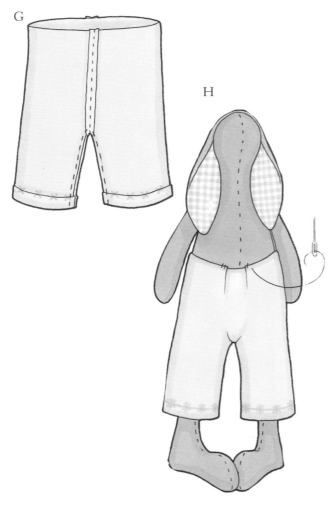

H

Match the centre seams and sew the leg seams, see Figure G.

Turn and press the pantaloons and fold in the seam allowance around the waist. If you have not yet hemmed the legs, press up the seam allowance, insert iron-on tape and press to hold. Then add the embroidery.

Put the pantaloons on the figure, making small tucks at the waist if necessary. Stitch the pantaloons to the body, see Figure H.

## PINAFORE DRESS

The measurements for the dress skirt are given below. These correspond to one skirt piece:

Large bunny – 20.5cm (8in) wide, 18cm (7in) deep.

Small bunny – 14.5cm (5¼in) wide, 13cm (5⅛in) deep.

Cut two skirt pieces to the measurements given above and a bib according to the pattern for the figure. Add seam allowances at the top and bottom of the skirt pieces, and all around the bib.

Press in the seam allowance at the top and on each side of the bib. Hold them in place using iron-on tape and iron to bond.

With right sides together place the bib centrally on one of the skirt pieces and sew it on, see Figure I. Press the bib up.

Add any machine embroidery at this stage. An embroidered heart has been added to the small bunny's dress just below the bib, see Figure J. Place the dress skirt pieces with right sides together and sew together up the sides. Press side seams open and then turn up the hem along the bottom and fix using iron-on tape. Press down the seam allowance at the top without fixing with tape.

Turn inside out. Hand or machine embroider along the bottom of the dress, if you wish.

I

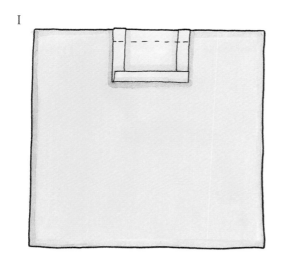

J

## STRAPS

Fold the dress fabric in half and place the pattern for the straps along the fold. Cut out two straps and sew along the long and one short edge, see Figures K and L. Turn the straps inside out and press.

Put the dress on the figure. Stitch two tucks at the front of the dress, one on each side of the bib, and two at the back, so the skirt fits the body. Place the stitched ends of the straps on the front of the bib and attach by hand sewing crosses or buttons, see Figure M. Cross the straps at the back, tuck the open ends inside the skirt and stitch to hold.

M

K

L

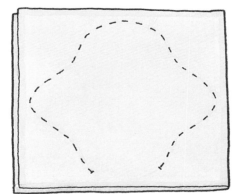

**N**

**HAT**

Fold the fabric for the hat double with right sides together, trace the pattern and sew around it, leaving an opening, see Figure N.

Cut out, turn inside out and press. Fold the half of the hat with the opening into the other half and press, see Figure O.

Embroider around the inner edge of the hat before pressing the brim up at the front and down at the back, see Figure P. Pull the hat firmly on to the head and add a few stitches at the neck and on each side.

**O**

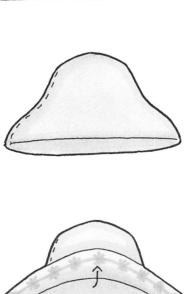

**P**

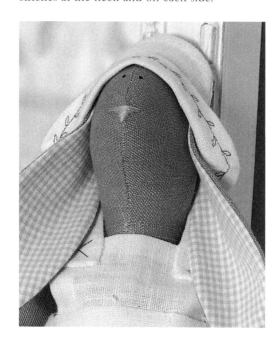

# PLAY TIME

## YOU WILL NEED
- *White or sand-coloured linen for the body*
- *Fabric for lining the ears*
- *Thin steel wire for the ears*
- *Fabric for clothes*
- *Stuffing*
- *Fabric paints and embroidery threads for the face and clothes*

## HOW TO MAKE

### BODY

Read the section on 'Stuffed Forms' on pages 8–9 before starting. Follow the instructions on pages 22–24 to make the body, but make the ears as described below:

Place a piece of linen fabric and a piece of ear lining fabric with right sides together. Trace two ears from the pattern and sew around the edges, see Figure A. Cut out and turn the ears inside out. Fold in the seam allowance at the bottom of each ear and press them. Shape two pieces of steel wire into approximately the shape of the ears and push them into each ear. The shaped wire should be longer than the ears, so that about 2cm (¾in) of each end of the wire stick out of the ears.

A

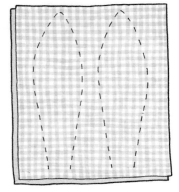

Use the patterns to make these playful bunnies in two sizes as shown.

Push the wire ends into the stuffed head of the hare and tack the ears on to the head, see Figure B. Bend the tops of the ears over as shown.

## PANTALOONS

Fold the fabric in half and place the straight edge of the pattern piece on the fold. Cut out two pieces for the pantaloons, adding extra seam allowance at the waist and at the bottom of the legs.

Place the two pieces with right sides together, and sew the centre seams, see Figure C.

If you want machine embroidery at the bottom of the legs, fold up the hem and use the embroidery to fasten it before you sew the leg seam. Make sure the embroidery is on the right side, see Figure D. If you do not want any embroidery, or if you are adding hand-sewn decorations, leave the hems until you have sewn up the trouser legs.

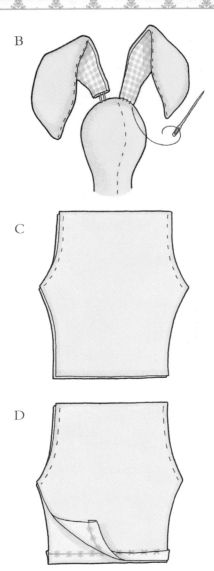

B

C

D

Match the centre seams and sew the leg seams, see Figure E.

Turn and press the pantaloons and fold in the seam allowance around the waist. If you have not yet hemmed the legs, press up the seam allowance, insert iron-on tape and press to hold. Then add the embroidery.

Put the pantaloons on the figure, making small tucks at the waist if necessary. Stitch the pantaloons to the body.

E

## PINAFORE DRESS

The measurements for the dress skirt are given below. These correspond to one skirt piece:

Large bunny – 20.5cm (8in) wide, 18cm (7in) deep.

Small bunny – 14.5cm (5¾in) wide, 13cm (5⅛in) deep.

Cut two skirt pieces to the measurements given above and a bib according to the pattern for the figure. Add seam allowances at the top and bottom of the skirt pieces, and all around the bib.

Press in the seam allowance at the top and on each side of the bib and hold them in place using iron-on tape and iron to bond.

With right sides together place the bib centrally on one of the skirt pieces and sew it on, see Figure G. Press the bib up.

Add any machine embroidery at this stage. An embroidered heart has been added to the large bunny's dress just below the bib, see Figure G. Place the skirt pieces with right sides together and sew together up the sides. Press side seams open and then turn up the hem along the bottom and fix using iron-on tape. Press down the seam allowance at the top without fixing with tape.

Turn inside out. Hand or machine embroider along the bottom of the dress, if you wish.

F

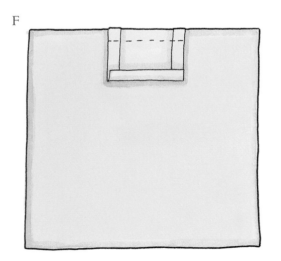

G

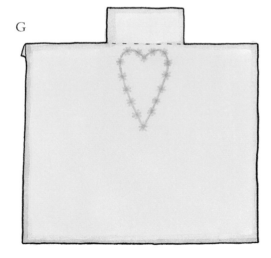

## STRAPS

Fold the dress fabric in half and place the pattern
for the straps along the fold. Cut out two straps
and sew along the long and one short edge,
see Figures H and I. Turn the straps inside out
and press.

Put the dress on the figure. Stitch two tucks
at the front of the dress, one on each side of the
bib, and two at the back, so the skirt fits the body.
Place the stitched ends of the straps on the front
of the bib and attach by hand sewing crosses or
buttons. Cross the straps at the back, tuck the
open ends inside the skirt and stitch to hold.

H

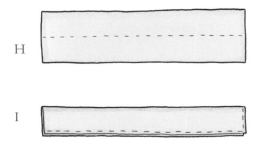

I

*These bunnies make perfect gifts or
can be used to decorate your home.*

# HIDE AND SEEK

- *White or sand-coloured linen for the body*
- *Fabric for lining the ears*
- *Thin steel wire for the ears*
- *Stuffing*
- *Fabric paints and embroidery threads for the face and clothes*
- *Flower pots*
- *Thin twigs and small beads to decorate the pot*

## HOW TO MAKE

### HEAD AND BODY

Make the head and body following the instructions for the Lazy Days bunnies on pages 22–24, without adding arms and legs. Tack the body across the bottom and put it into a flower pot.

### DECORATING THE POT

Decorate the top of the pot with twigs held in place around the edge with a glue gun. Thread beads on to thin steel wire and wind them around the twigs.

Decorate the outside of the pot with a heart, tracing round the pattern. Paint the outline of the heart using a fine paintbrush, then stamp the dots using the large and small heads of pins. Start by placing the large dots evenly along the painted line and then surround these dots with six smaller dots.

Create these cute flowerpot companions by simply sewing the body and ears.

# BUNNY APPLIQUÉ

## YOU WILL NEED

- *Various fabrics*
- *Double sided iron-on interfacing*
- *White fabric paint*
- *Flat brush (size 6–8)*
- *Fabric paints for the face and embroidery threads*
- *Lightweight fusible interfacing*
- *Lining fabric for the back*
- *Wadding*
- *Fabrics for the appliqué*
- *Fabric paints for the face and embroidery threads*

## HOW TO MAKE

### APPLIQUÉ DECORATIONS

The pattern pieces for the appliqué decorations are reversed because the outlines are traced on the wrong side of the fabric. When the figures are turned around, they will match the decorations shown in the pictures.

Place double sided iron-on interfacing on the wrong side of the fabric and press to bond. Remove the backing paper.

Trace the outlines of the pattern pieces on to the wrong side (the glue side) of the bonded fabric and cut out. Place the pieces on a sheet of paper, card or acetate film with the right side up.

The appliqué is brushed with fabric paint to give it an appealing finish.

Look at the pictures of the appliqué decorations to see where the painted effect is placed on the figures. Dip a dry brush into the fabric paint and dab off the excess on a piece of paper. Brush the paint on to the pieces, moving the brush quickly back and forth. Leave to dry then repeat the process if the effect is too weak.

If the edges of the fabric have frayed a little, wait until the paint is dry and then trim the edge with sharp, pointed scissors.

Place the appliqué pieces on the background fabric, starting with the lowest piece and iron them on.

The head of the hare and labels are outlined with a neat running stitch using a contrasting thread. Blanket stitch around the mugs and teapot by hand or with a sewing machine. Add a line of running stitches for the coil of 'steam'.

The words on the labels are sewn using long straight stitches. Draw them using a washable marker pen before stitching. You could practise first on an acetate sheet and then transfer the words on to the fabric.

Decorate the faces on the figures as described on page 8.

## POTHOLDERS

Iron fusible interfacing to the wrong side of the front fabric pieces to get a firm base for the appliqué.

Cut out a piece of front fabric, a piece of lining fabric and two pieces of wadding each measuring 17 × 23cm (6¾ × 9in), adding seam allowances. Cut a strip of fabric measuring 4 × 11cm (1¾ × 4⅓in) without seam allowance for the loop. Press just under 1cm (½in) to the wrong side along each of the long sides, see Figure A. Then fold the strip in half, matching the edges of the folds, and sew along the long side, see Figure B.

Place two layers of wadding on the wrong side of the fabric lining and zigzag stitch around the edge to fasten the wadding to the fabric.

Appliqué the decoration on to the front of the fabric as described on pages 38–40. Place the appliquéd fabric piece and the lining with right sides together. Place the loop between the fabric and the lining at the top of the potholder and sew around the edge, leaving an opening at the bottom for turning it inside out. See Figure C.

Trim any excess seam allowance and turn the potholder inside out. Fold in the seam allowance at the opening and sew it up. Press the potholder and then sew a seam about 6mm (¼in) in from the edge with the sewing machine, see Figure D.

A

B

C

D

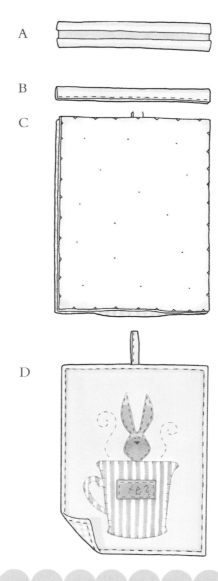

41

## TEA COSY

Trace the tea cosy pattern so that the dotted lines between A and B match each other. Fold the fabric, lining and interfacing in half and place the centre line of the pattern on the folds of the fabrics, see Figure A.

Cut out two pieces of fabric, two pieces of lining and four pieces of heavyweight interfacing or two pieces of lightweight interfacing and two pieces of wadding according to the pattern, adding seam allowances.

Iron two layers of heavyweight interfacing to the wrong side of each fabric piece. Sew around with zigzag stitches to keep the layers in place.

If you are using wadding first iron lightweight fusible interfacing to the wrong side of each of the two fabric pieces. Then add the wadding to each piece and sew around with zigzag stitches.

Appliqué the hare and teapot decoration on one of the fabric pieces, see pages 38–40.

Place each fabric piece right sides together with a lining piece. Sew them together along the curved bottom edge, see Figure B. Trim to leave about 7–8mm (⅜in) seam allowance along the curve to make a neat edge at the bottom of the cosy. Make a loop in the same way as for the potholders.

Open out the fabric and lining pieces and place the two parts of the tea cosy with right sides together. Make sure the seams along the curved bottom edges match. Place the loop between the two layers of fabric at the top and sew around leaving an opening for turning inside out in the lining, see Figure C.

A

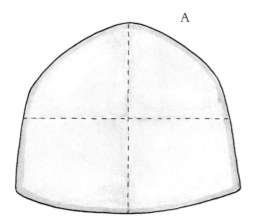

B

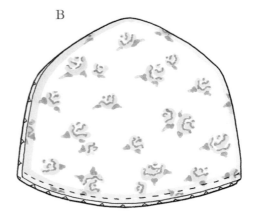

Cut off the excess seam allowance around the tea cosy. Press the seam allowance between the lining and the fabric towards the lining. Turn the tea cosy inside out and sew up the opening.

Push the lining into the tea cosy. The seam allowance between the fabric and the lining makes a decorative edge at the bottom of the tea cosy. Press the tea cosy, making sure the bottom border edge is even.

C

*Try using a patterned fabric for your tea cosy to create a bolder look.*

# EASTER CARDS

## YOU WILL NEED

- *Card blanks or a selection of thin sheets of card*
- *Fabrics*
- *Iron-on fusible tape*
- *Double-sided adhesive foam tabs*
- *Raffia strips for the bow*
- *Ribbons*
- *Fine brown marking pen*
- *Fabric paints for the face*
- *Hole punch*

## HOW TO MAKE

### CARDS

The backing panel and the largest egg are made from fabric and attached directly to the card with iron-on fusible tape. Do not use too hot an iron or the card will wrinkle. Sew a zigzag edging around the panel and the egg with a sewing machine.

Cut out the bunny's head and small egg from card. You can draw a line of stitches around the head with a pen. Cut out and glue on a little nose. Make the rest of the face as described on page 8.

Glue the bunny's head and the small egg on the card with double-sided tabs. Tie a raffia bow and glue it on the bunny. Make a hole through both layers of the card with a hole punch. When you have written the card, you can tie it on with a piece of ribbon.

These cards measure 16 × 16cm (6¼ × 6¼in), but you could also make smaller gift tags to match.

# SUPPLIERS

## UK

Panduro Hobby
Westway House
Transport Avenue
Brentford
Middlesex
TW8 9HF
Tel: 020 8566 1680
trade@panduro.co.uk
www.pandurohobby.co.uk

Coast and Country
Crafts & Quilts
8 Sampson Gardens
Ponsanooth, Truro
Cornwall
TR3 7RS
Tel: 01872 863894
www.coastandcountrycrafts.co.uk

Fred Aldous Ltd.
37 Lever Street
Manchester
M1 1LW
Tel: 08707 517301
www.fredaldous.co.uk

The Sewing Bee
52 Hillfoot Street
Dunoon, Argyll
PA23 7DT
Tel: 01369 706879
www.thesewingbee.co.uk

Puddlecrafts
7 St. Clair Park
Route Militaire
St. Sampson
Guernsey
GY2 4DX
Tel: 01481 245441
www.puddlecrafts.co.uk

The Fat Quarters
5 Choprell Road
Blackhall Mill
Newcastle
NE17 7TN
Tel: 01207 565728
www.thefatquarters.co.uk

Threads and Patches
48 Aylesbury Street
Fenny Stratford
Bletchley
Milton Keynes
MK2 2BU
Tel: 01908 649687
www.threadsandpatches.co.uk

## USA

Coats and Clark USA
PO Box 12229
Greenville
SC29612-0229
Tel: 0800 648 1479
www.coatsandclark.com

Connecting Threads
13118 NE 4th Street
Vancouver
WA 9884
www.connectingthreads.com

eQuilter.com
5455 Spine Road, Suite E
Boulder
CO 80301
www.equilter.com

Hamels Fabrics
5843 Lickman Road
Chilliwack
British Columbia
V2R 4B5
www.hamelsfabrics.com

Keepsake Quilting
Box 1618 Center Harbor
NH 03226
www.keepsakequilting.com

The Craft Connection
21055 Front Street
PO Box 1088
Onley
VA 23418
www.craftconn.com

# INDEX

# TEMPLATES

All templates need to be enlarged by 400%.
Add seam allowance for all templates, except
for the appliqué shapes and card motifs.

## Hide and Seek
(page 36)

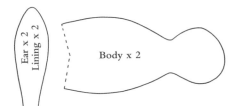

Ear x 2
Lining x 2

Body x 2

## Bunny Appliqué
(page 38)

Fabric x 2
Lining x 2
Fusible interfacing x 2

B        B

Place on fold

A        A

tid for tea?

tea?

time

# On the Farm
(page 16)

Dress x 2

Pocket x 1

Dungarees x 2

Body x 2

Ears x 2

Carrot x 2

Back piece x 1

Arm x 4

Sun hat x 2

# Easter Cards
(page 44)

Card motifs

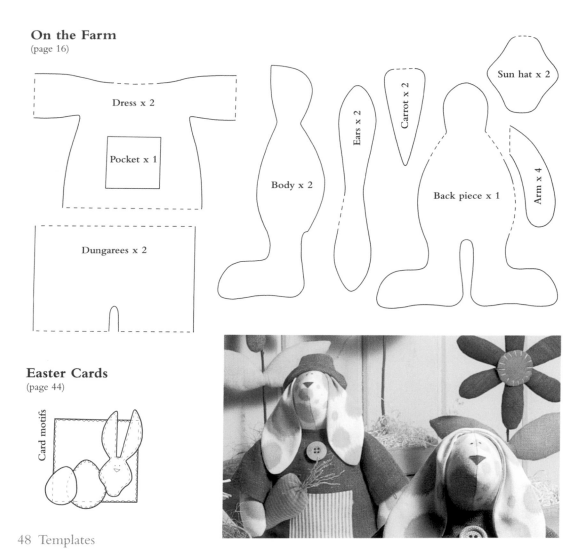

# Lazy Days and Play Time
(page 22)        (page 30)

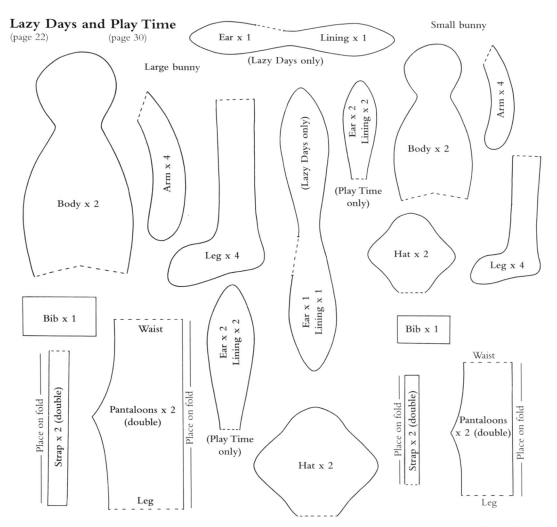

Ear x 1        Lining x 1

(Lazy Days only)

Small bunny

Large bunny

Ear x 2
Lining x 2

Arm x 4

Arm x 4

(Lazy Days only)

(Play Time only)

Body x 2

Body x 2

Leg x 4

Hat x 2

Leg x 4

Bib x 1

Ear x 1
Lining x 1

Bib x 1

Place on fold

Strap x 2 (double)

Waist

Pantaloons x 2
(double)

Place on fold

Ear x 2
Lining x 2

(Play Time
only)

Hat x 2

Place on fold

Strap x 2 (double)

Waist

Pantaloons
x 2 (double)

Place on fold

Leg

Leg